CRIMINAL SOVEREIGNTY:
UNDERSTANDING NORTH KOREA'S
ILLICIT INTERNATIONAL ACTIVITIES

Paul Rexton Kan
Bruce E. Bechtol, Jr.
Robert M. Collins

March 2010

*****

Originally published by the Strategic Studies Institute.

*****

Comments pertaining to this report are invited and should be forwarded to: Director, Strategic Studies Institute, U.S. Army War College, 122 Forbes Ave, Carlisle, PA 17013-5244.

*****

All Strategic Studies Institute (SSI) publications are available on the SSI homepage for electronic dissemination free of charge. Hard copies of this report may also be ordered from our homepage free of charge. SSI's homepage address is: *www. StrategicStudiesInstitute.army.mil*.

*****

Cover and promotional text (c) Booklife 2011
ISBN 978-1-257-11778-9

FOREWORD

The authors of this monograph have exposed a key piece of the puzzle which helps to provide a better understanding of North Korea's surreptitious international behavior. For years, North Korea's military provocations have been obvious to the world, however, much of its decisionmaking is shrouded in secrecy, particularly that of a wide-range of clandestine activities. This monograph is unique in the way that it sheds light on the illicit activities of the regime, and how those illegal activities are used to support its military programs and the government itself.

From drug trafficking to counterfeiting, from money laundering to cigarette smuggling, North Korea's Central Committee Bureau 39 is an active participant in the criminal economy of the region with tentacles extending well beyond Asia. The authors discuss how these activities have negative strategic consequences for a number of stakeholders and nations throughout the region while describing how such activities provide critical funding streams for military programs and regime supporters.

As a result, North Korea is not just a "rogue state," but practices what is essentially criminal sovereignty whereby it organizes its illegitimate activities behind the shield of non-intervention while using the tools of the state to perpetrate these schemes abroad. The authors argue that this arrangement has important links to succession issues within the regime. They also argue that policy makers who are concerned with the development of future policies and strategies aimed toward North Korea must view those new policies from a different perspective than that used in the past.

DOUGLAS C. LOVELACE, JR.
Director
Strategic Studies Institute

ABOUT THE AUTHORS

PAUL REXTON KAN is currently an Associate Professor of National Security Studies at the U.S. Army War College at Carlisle, Pennsylvania. His previous assignment was the Deputy Director of the Center for China-United States Cooperation where he coordinated professional exchanges with Chinese officials from the policy institutions linked to the Ministry of Foreign Affairs, the Ministry of State Security, and the People's Liberation Army. Dr. Kan is the author of the recent book, *Drugs and Contemporary Warfare* (Dulles, VA: Potomac Books, 2009); and "Drugging Babylon: The Illegal Narcotics Trade and Nation-Building in Iraq, " in *Small Wars and Insurgencies* (June 2007). His research on Mexican cartel violence will be part of an upcoming book on the subject, and he is currently working on his next book, "Whiskey Rebellions, Opium Wars, and Other Battles for Intoxication." Dr. Kan holds a Ph.D. in International Studies from the Graduate School of International Studies at the University of Denver.

BRUCE E. BECHTOL, JR., is a Professor of International Relations at the Marine Corps Command and Staff College. His previous assignments include: a faculty member of the Air Command and Staff College, an adjunct Visiting Professor at the Korea University Graduate School of International Studies, and an adjunct Professor of Diplomacy at Norwich University. He was an Intelligence Officer at the Defense Intelligence Agency, eventually serving as the Senior Analyst for Northeast Asia in the Intelligence Directorate (J2) on the Joint Staff in the Pentagon. Before beginning his career at the Defense Intelligence Agency, he was on active duty for 20 years in the

U.S. Marine Corps, serving at various locations in the western Pacific and East Asia. Formerly the Editor of the *Defense Intelligence Journal*, Dr. Bechtol also sat on the Editorial Review Board of the *East Asian Review*. He has written widely on Korean security issues, contributing articles to such journals as the *International Journal of Korean Studies*, *Pacific Focus*, *Contemporary Strategy*, *Foreign Policy*, the *Korea Observer*, *East Asian Review*, the *Air and Space Power Journal*, the *International Journal of Korean Unification Studies*, *Korean Quarterly*, and *Occasional Papers: The Journal of the Korea American Historical Society*. In addition to serving on the Board of Directors of the International Council on Korean Studies, Dr. Bechtol sits on the Board of Directors of the Council on U.S.-Korean Security Studies. He is the author of *Defiant Failed State: The North Korean Threat to International Security* (Dulles, VA: Potomac Books, 2010), *Red Rogue: The Persistent Challenge of North Korea* (Dulles, VA: Potomac Books, 2007), and the editor of *The Quest for a Unified Korea: Strategies for the Cultural and Interagency Process* (Quantico, VA: Marine Corps University Foundation, 2007). Dr. Bechtol holds a Ph.D. from the Union Institute.

ROBERT COLLINS is a retired political analyst with 37 years in the Department of Defense. His focus is on Korean and Northeast Asian security issues. He served for 31 years in South Korea with United States Forces Korea and the Combined Forces Command. Mr. Collins holds a Master's Degree in International Relations from Dankook University, Seoul, Korea.

SUMMARY

North Korea's criminal conduct—smuggling, trafficking, and counterfeiting—is well known, but the organization directing it is understudied or overlooked. Policymakers, military leaders, and scholars may feel that they have a reasonable grasp on how and why North Korea is actively involved in criminal enterprises. However, unlike the other remaining communist states "orphaned" after the Cold War, or ordinary corrupt autocratic regimes, or criminally linked warlords and insurgent groups, North Korea practices a form of "criminal sovereignty" that is unique in the contemporary international security arena. North Korea uses state sovereignty to protect itself from external interference in its domestic affairs while dedicating a portion of its government to carrying out illicit international activities in defiance of international law and the domestic laws of numerous other nations. The proceeds of these activities are then used in a number of ways to sustain North Korea's existence and to enable other policies. For example, criminal proceeds are distributed to members of the North Korean elite (including senior officers of the armed forces); are used to support Kim Jong-il's personal life style; and are invested in its military apparatus.

The authors of this monograph focus on North Korea's Office #39 as the state apparatus that directs illicit activities to include the manufacture and distribution of illegal drugs, the counterfeiting of U.S. currency, and the manufacture and distribution of counterfeit cigarettes. Finally, as Kim Jong-Il becomes more frail, the authors assess how his successor may continue or alter Office #39's activities.

CRIMINAL SOVEREIGNTY: UNDERSTANDING NORTH KOREA'S ILLICIT INTERNATIONAL ACTIVITIES

North Korea's leadership is able to persistently ratchet up tensions in the region due to its ability to gain funding from a vast array of illicit international enterprises organized by a part of its government known as Central Committee Bureau 39 (also known as Office #39) of the Korean Workers' Party (KWP). This shadowy part of an already opaque government is only briefly mentioned in the analysis of North Korea's international behavior or foreign policy. North Korea's criminal conduct—smuggling, trafficking, and counterfeiting—is well known, but the organization directing it is understudied or overlooked. The authors of this monograph (two of whom have worked for the U.S. Government in roles directly scrutinizing North Korea's behavior) have relied on interviews with defectors, congressional testimony from aid workers working within the country, and press reports from around Asia to fill this void. Shedding some light on the nature and activities of Office #39 is essential in developing appropriate responses to an increasingly bellicose regime that is threatening regional stability.

Policymakers, military leaders, and scholars may feel that they have a reasonable grasp on how and why North Korea is actively involved in criminal enterprises. North Korea's criminal schemes could be considered as a response to the demise of the Soviet Union, one of the regime's key benefactors. In 1990, the Soviet Union informed North Korea that any future imports would have to be paid for in hard currency (at the world price), and requested repayment of Pyongyang's $4 billion in debt.[1] After all, the other remaining communist regimes of Cuba, Vietnam, Laos,

1

and China each have very well developed and active criminal syndicates that operate across a number of borders. But none of these communist hold-outs directs a portion of their government to engage in criminal acts as a matter of regime survival. Furthermore, Office #39 was started in 1974, well before the end of the Cold War.

North Korea may appear to have the familiar outlines of a typical corrupt autocratic regime, but it is different. It is unlike other autocratic states whose leaders turn a blind eye to criminal acts within their own territory, preside over a bloated bureaucracy to accrue bribes and kickbacks, or receive a cut from the profits of domestic organized crime groups. "Unlike Latin America or Europe, where organized crime attempts to penetrate the state, North Korea is penetrating organized crime."[2] The crimes organized by Office #39 are committed beyond the borders of North Korea by the regime itself, not solely for the personal enrichment of the leadership, but to prop up its armed forces and to fund its military programs.

In this way, North Korea may be compared to cases of warlord criminality as practiced in countries like Sierra Leone, Liberia, Congo, Sudan, and Myanmar (Burma), or criminally financed insurgent groups like the Revolutionary Armed Forces of Colombia (FARC), or the Taliban in Afghanistan. These groups also engage in wide ranging illegal activities to keep themselves viable in a hostile strategic and operational environment. In fact, North Korea sees itself as being surrounded by enemies who are bent on eliminating it.[3] Once again, however, North Korea is different. It is a nation-state; Kim Jong-il is not a warlord, nor is the KWP or Office #39 an insurgent group. To commit its criminal acts, Office #39 uses the powers and resources of a nation-state—merchant and military vessels, diplomatic and embassy posts, as well as state run companies and collective farms—that nonstate groups do not possess.

Unlike the other remaining communist states "orphaned" after the Cold War, or ordinary corrupt autocratic regimes, or criminally linked warlords and insurgent groups, North Korea practices a form of "criminal sovereignty" that is unique in the contemporary international security arena. North Korea uses state sovereignty to protect itself from external interference in its domestic affairs while dedicating a portion of its government and the KWP to carrying out illicit international activities in defiance of international law and the domestic laws of numerous other nations. Criminal sovereignty means that rather than the Weberian notion of the state maintaining the monopoly on the legitimate use of force, the state, in the case of North Korea, maintains the monopoly on the conduct of illicit activities. Furthermore, unlike other states that use their national instruments of power of diplomacy, law enforcement, and military force to combat international crimes, North Korea directs its national instruments of power to *commit* crimes in other states. The proceeds of these activities are then used in a number of ways to sustain North Korea's existence and to enable other policies. For example, criminal proceeds are distributed to members of the North Korean elite (including senior officers of the armed forces); they support Kim Jong-il's personal life style; and are invested in its military apparatus. North Korea is, as others have called it, a "Soprano State."[4]

Such unique international behavior requires a more meaningful examination of Office #39's origins, organizational structure, and activities in order to develop a more calibrated strategy and policy to meet the North Korean challenge. This monograph will focus on Office #39's key illicit activities—to include manufacture and distribution of illegal drugs, the counterfeiting of U.S. currency, and the manufacture and distribution of counterfeit cigarettes. Finally, as Kim Jong-Il becomes more frail, the need to assess how his successor may continue or alter Office #39's activities grows more acute and will also be examined.

ORIGINS AND ACTIVITIES OF OFFICE #39

The emergence of criminal sovereignty began in the 1970s when the North Korean leadership realized it needed to increase the amount of funds coming in to support the government beyond the huge Soviet subsidies it was receiving at the time. Thus, reportedly in 1974, North Korea took action to establish an office to alleviate this problem.[5] To make criminal sovereignty functional, Office #39 was created as a department-level organization within the KWP Secretariat under the KWP Central Committee. The office was established for the explicit purpose of running illegal activities to generate currency for the North Korean government. Office #39 generated a slush fund under the exclusive guidance of Kim Il-sung's son—who later became the leader of North Korea—Kim Jong-il.[6] This also points to a key aspect of this program. It has been under the supervision and guidance of the younger Kim since its founding (and long before his father began to gradually hand over other elements of the government to his son before the elder Kim's death in 1994).[7] Office #39, also known as "the keeper of Kim's cashbox," lies completely outside the jurisdiction of the North Korean Government's cabinet and is separated from the cabinet's national economic planning process.[8] The headquarters for Office #39 sits in downtown Pyongyang, not far from Kim Jong-il's official office building, and very close to the Koryo Hotel—which is often frequented by foreign tourists. Through its offices in Pyongyang, it operates through government and KWP-run front companies such as Daesung Chongguk (which has been known to have offices in Austria), and Zokwang Trading Company (which has an office in Macao). All of the many front companies in the web that runs North Korea's diverse illicit activities answer directly to the building in Pyongyang that houses Office #39. This Office, in turn, answers directly to Kim Jong-il, who is known to often oversee the actual disbursement of funds derived from its many activities.[9]

In the past, Macao was one of the key operating centers for the companies that answer to Office #39, and was often seen as the center overseas point. In Macao, dozens of North Korean "merchants" holding diplomatic passports ran the nerve center for many of North Korea's operations in East Asia and other areas of the world for several years—keeping what worked out to be a de facto consulate running from the small island city. The diplomatic status of the North Koreans, combined with Macao's lax banking laws, made it relatively easy to literally launder suitcase loads of counterfeit money, or money earned from drug operations (among others) through banks in the former colony of Portugal. Pyongyang has also reportedly used these banks to deposit and/or exchange currency used in missile deals and other deals relating to weapons of mass destruction (WMD) projects that North Korea has proliferated in recent years.[10]

As shown in Figure 1, Office #39 sits at the top of a maze of operations, encompassing the party, the military, and an even hazier group of entities such as government backed front companies. Sometimes these front companies answer directly to other offices in the government or the KWP (who eventually answer to Office #39), and sometimes they answer to either military or party organizations.

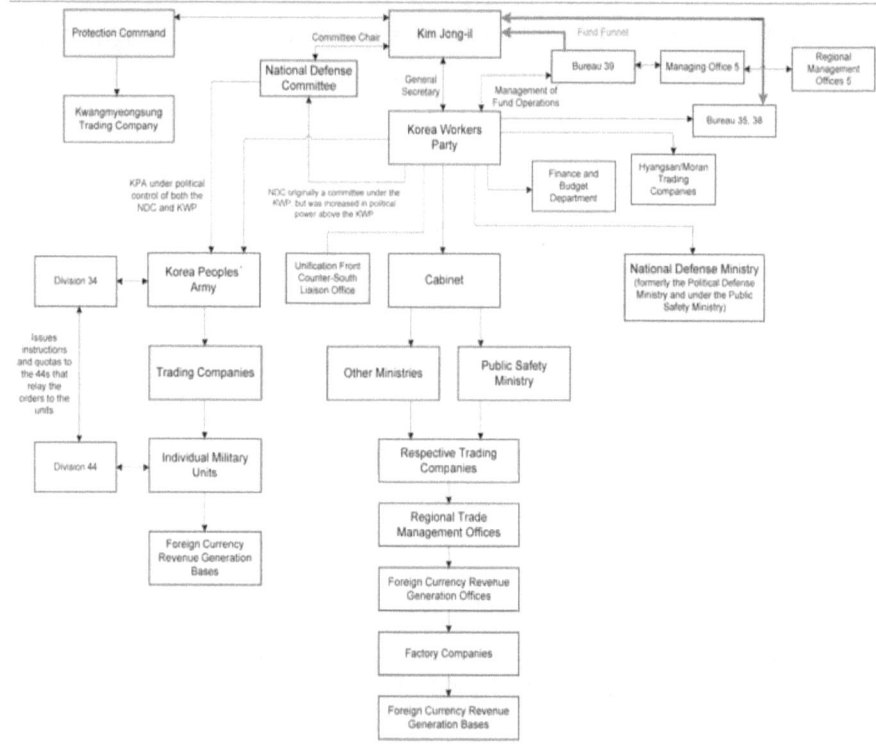

Source: John Park, "North Korea, Inc.: Gaining Insights into Regime Stability in North Korea From Recent Commercial Activities," *United States Institute of Peace Working Paper*, Washington, DC: United States Institute of Peace, 2009.

Figure 1. North Korea's Legal, Illegal, and Illicit Activities Network.

Kim Jong-il reportedly maintains a slush fund from these activities worth billions of dollars, and has used banks in Macao and banks in Switzerland (among others) in the past, to hide funds that can be used for whatever purpose is designated as being for the good of the people. Interviews conducted by reporters from the *Wall Street Journal* with intelligence officials in East Asia produced estimates that the slush fund generated by Office #39 amounted to hard currency in the vicinity of $5 billion.[11] Recent pressure from the U.S. Government on banks in Macao (beginning in 2005), and publicity regarding holdings in Switzerland, may have caused a number of the secret bank accounts to be moved to banks in Luxembourg.[12] During August 2006, other reports surfaced alleging Pyongyang had moved some of its monetary accounts to a bank in Singapore.[13] Events initiated by the U.S. Treasury Department caused Macao's banking regulators to freeze $25 million worth of North Korean accounts in the Banco Delta Asia, the most notable of the "Macao Connections" that the U.S. Government had singled out. Press reports indicated that Zokwang Trading Company, the primary front company for illicit activities centered in Macao, closed its headquarters on the fifth floor of an office building near Banco Delta Asia. Reportedly, most of its personnel have relocated to Zhuhai, just across the border in China proper.[14]

An analysis of the network that exists for North Korea's illicit activities shows that a plethora of front companies under the auspices of Office #39 have become the important moneymaking operation that is not only used for an illegal slush fund, but to sponsor a wide variety of actions the government and the KWP in Pyongyang would otherwise be too short of funds to accomplish. The line of control runs from Kim Jong-il, to the front companies, to the activities that they carry out, and then back to Kim Jong-il as the profits from these activities roll in. As the next section will demonstrate, this KWP operation has been ongoing since the mid-1970s (but has apparently increased in scope in the past 10 years), and its complexity shows that the North Korean regime is not only effective in conducting these activities through front companies and banks willing to launder their money, but they are also effective at keeping their operations covert.

Drug Trafficking.

Drug trafficking by Office #39 is another aspect of criminal sovereignty because it plays to North Korea's distinct advantages as a nation-state. While organized crime and terrorist and insurgent groups involved in drug trafficking must contend with circumventing state authority and avoiding interdiction at each node of the trafficking network, North Korea grows, manufactures, processes, warehouses, and transports drugs freely. North Korean refugees describe the country as a "narco-state in which all aspects of the drugs operation—from school children toiling in poppy fields to government-owned processing plants to state-owned cargo ships and trading companies—are controlled by Kim [Jong-Il]."[15] In short, there is no government to circumvent; in fact, the state itself actively participates in all levels of drug production within the country. "State collective farms and youth brigades [are] used to produce opium to earn hard currency. Villages had to meet production targets, and the military helped with distribution."[16] According to North Korean defector Kim Young-il, North Korea began its illicit drug production in earnest during the late 1970s, and opium produced on farms is sent to pharmaceutical plants in the Nanam area of Chongjin in Hamkyong Bukto Province where it is processed into heroin.[17] International aid workers assisting North Korea during its famine in the 1990s reveal the level of state penetration in heroin production.

We could not figure out why farmers that I interviewed said they had a third of their land in their villages not farmed. There is a certain Korean word they used, "Pomyong." Recently, we learned that the term in North Korea means the land is put aside for poppy production. They shrewdly substituted a word for "fallow land" for poppy production. So it is actually state-managed, state-run, and there is an allocation made in state farms for actually producing poppy. It is not illegal. It is encouraged.[18]

State-supported drug production, however, is not for domestic consumption. The major narcotics that North Korea produces are heroin and methamphetamine, which are exported around the region and around the globe. North Korea must still circumvent international law and domestic laws of other countries to turn a profit. Once again, North Korea is able to leverage its powers as a nation-state to aid circumvention. Office #39 facilitates the international distribution of narcotics by using national assets such as military and commercial vessels for transportation, diplomatic personnel to sell to wholesale markets, and state-owned businesses to launder the profits to escape seizure. The depth and scope of North Korea's trafficking capabilities can be seen in the examples of interdiction that have occurred over the years.

Much of the drug transportation to the wholesale drug markets run by underworld groups is done with North Korean ocean-going vessels. North Korean ships have been known to rendezvous with Japanese vessels in North Korean territorial waters to transfer narcotics. However, North Korean military vessels have ventured in other territorial waters to conduct drug drops. In 2001, the Japanese Coast Guard and a North Korean ship exchanged fire, resulting in the sinking of the North Korean naval vessel that was operated by North Korean special forces. Japanese authorities subsequently determined that the North Korean ship entered Japanese waters to deliver meth-amphetamines to Japanese Yakuza members.[19] In the following year, Taiwanese authorities stopped and searched a Taiwanese fishing trawler which contained 174 pounds of heroin that it had received from a North Korean gunboat.[20] In 2003, Australian police arrested three men in a coastal village west of Melbourne who had received $50 million of street-ready heroin from a dinghy launched by the state owned North Korean ship, *Pong Su*, which lay just off shore. North Korea has used its merchant fleet to act as a middleman for other groups involved in drug trafficking by bartering other goods, such as weapons, in exchange for drugs. A North Korean vessel laden with small arms was detained by authorities in Myanmar who believed that local insurgent groups were intent on trading heroin for the arms.[21]

North Korea has also used its diplomatic corps to aid the transport of drugs directly to wholesale markets that lie in specific countries. This was particularly evident in the 1990s, but stretches as far back as the 1970s. In 1977, after only 3 years of diplomatic ties, Venezuela expelled all North Korean diplomats for trafficking drugs.[22] In 1996, Russia arrested a North Korean envoy with 50 pounds of heroin in his possession.[23] In 1998, Egyptian police arrested a North Korean diplomat who was attempting to smuggle 500,000 tabs of rohypnol (also known as the "date rape drug") into Egypt while Russian authorities arrested two North Korean diplomats in possession of 35 kilograms of cocaine.[24] Later the same year, German police arrested the North Korean deputy ambassador who possessed heroin that was believed to be manufactured in North Korea, and Chinese authorities arrested a North Korean consulate employee with 9 kilograms of opium.[25]

However, with the exposure of its use of diplomatic personnel for distribution of drugs to the wholesale market, North Korea was forced to adapt by outsourcing this portion of drug trafficking to organized criminal groups such as the Yakuza.[26] Once again, North Korea was able to take advantage of its power as a nation-state.

For criminal organizations, a state partner offers a steady supply of high quality drugs, escape from the inefficiencies associated with avoiding enforcement, and resources exceeding those of a typical nonstate group. For North Korea, this arrangement balances risk reduction with satisfactory profit, capitalizing on the state's competitive advantage in creating an enforcement-free production environment, eliminating competition over distribution, and obtaining cover of plausible deniability.[27]

Such partnering with organized crime has reduced North Korea's exposure to interdiction efforts, and has led several countries like the United States, China, and Russia to focus on how to trace and intercept the regime's proceeds. North Korea's ties to organized crime in Asia, and elsewhere, appear to be both diverse and extensive. They have reportedly engaged in sophisticated drug drops at sea with the Yakuza from Japan (using Special Operations Forces).[28] North Korean drug smuggling has also been linked to the Russian Mafiya and other organizations in Europe and Southeast Asia.[29] Pyongyang has even been establishing links with Taiwanese organized crime syndicates—reportedly inviting members to North Korea for meetings.[30]

Receiving and laundering the proceeds of drug trafficking has largely been done through foreign banks in China, Switzerland, and Luxembourg. However, North Korean banks, namely Banco Delta Asia, have been at the forefront. The Macao branch of the bank has faced ever growing scrutiny by the international community and tighter controls by Chinese authorities. As previously discussed, $25 million of the bank's assets in Macao were frozen in 2005, and more stringent requirements for opening of new accounts appear to be taking their toll.[31] In an effort to avoid further scrutiny and tighter controls, it appears that Office #39 has once again turned to North Korea's diplomatic corps. In February 2006, North Korean diplomats were caught smuggling $1 million and 200 million yen in cash into Mongolia.[32]

Counterfeit Currency Operations.

North Korea's long history of illegal drug manufacture and sales all over Asia has now become fairly well known. But until recent years, one of its other sources of hard currency for Kim Jong-il's slush fund was not as well known—counterfeit currency. Part of the 2005 action undertaken by the U.S. Government against banks in Macao was to staunch Office #39's laundering of counterfeit United States $100 bills.[33] The U.S. Secret Service has said on several occasions that the North Korean-manufactured counterfeit U.S. $100 bills currently in circulation are the most sophisticated in the world (thus leading to their widely used nickname—"Supernotes").[34]

North Korea's counterfeit currency operations are extremely sophisticated and run by skilled experts. According to press reports, high-tech equipment from Japan was acquired to manufacture the bills, as well as paper from Hong Kong and ink from France. By 1989, millions of dollars of this fake American currency was being distributed worldwide. It is probably important to point out at this point that North Korea is the only government in the world known to be running a counterfeit money operation as a matter of state policy.[35] The North Korean counterfeit distribution network includes diplomats, Chinese gangsters, organized crime syndicates in Asia and elsewhere (possibly Russia), banks (especially in Macao), and criminals associated with the Irish Republican Army.[36] Defectors alleged in 2005 that a factory in the city of Pyeongseong prints the counterfeit $100 bills—and this assessment was also supported by recent travelers to North Korea and China. According to press reports, the bills have often been exchanged with Chinese merchants at 50 percent of their value and then mixed in with real bills.[37]

North Korean intelligence services have reportedly used the Supernotes to finance activities overseas, and even for foreign purchases made on behalf of Kim Jong-il. The counterfeit U.S. banknotes were discovered in Manila, the Philippines, in 1989, and months later were also unearthed in Belgrade, Serbia. The bills have also surfaced in a diverse set of places such as Ethiopia, Peru, Germany, and once again, Macao.[38] The bills have even surfaced in Lebanon's Bekka Valley.[39] According to Yonhap, the semi-official information arm of the South Korean government, the number of bogus U.S. bills detected in the country has increased since 2005—again mostly in $100 bills, and again, likely from North Korea.[40] The Supernotes have even surfaced in Las Vegas, Nevada—reportedly first during 2005. In 2007 a Chinese businessman was arrested there who was apparently using the casinos to help launder the bills that he had acquired from the North Koreans. The bills have also been linked to North Korea's WMD proliferation—as reportedly they are sometimes used in transactions.[41]

In 2006, a 3-month investigation by the Chinese government, of accusations that North Korea was using banks in Macao to launder counterfeit profits, confirmed suspicions raised by the U.S. Government. South Korean diplomats revealed to the press that Chinese officials had expressed their concerns regarding the counterfeiting of U.S. currency to a North Korean delegation during a visit to Beijing, China, by Kim Kye-kwan (a highly placed North Korean diplomat holding the title of Vice Foreign Minister).[42] North Korean counterfeit U.S. bank notes reportedly surfaced in Hong Kong during February 2006.[43] In what was probably an indicator of concern in Beijing, in March 2006, the Peoples Bank of China issued a directive to financial institutions to "increase vigilance" against fake $100 bills.[44]

Counterfeit Cigarettes.

North Korea's illicit and illegal drug production and marketing, and its counterfeiting of American currency, have been the focus of attention in recent years; but another aspect of Pyongyang's illicit activities is also highly profitable—counterfeit cigarettes. Because of the nature of the product, counterfeit cigarettes are easily exportable through both front companies and legal shipping means. In fact, counterfeit cigarettes may be North Korea's largest and most profitable container export. Large tobacco corporations based in the United States, Japan, and South Korea used private investigations to identify factories in North Korea producing counterfeit cigarettes and have worked with officials from both their own countries and others in the region to stop the distribution of the contraband. The overhead for the smuggling of these "fake" cigarettes is very low. According to former State Department official David Asher, a standard 40-foot container full of counterfeit cigarettes may cost as little as $70,000 to produce but have a street value of $3 to $4 million. These operations apparently picked up in scope and focus almost from the beginning of the Kim Jong-il regime. An example is the 1995 incident, that the Associated Press reported, when authorities in Taiwan seized 20 containers on a ship bound for North Korea that were full of counterfeit cigarette wrappers that at the time would have rendered a street value of up to $1 billion in cigarettes.[45]

Defector testimony has revealed that there are counterfeit cigarette factories that are located in several areas in North Korea — all, of course, off limits to foreigners. According to Park Syung-je of the Korean Military Analysts Association, at least one of these factories reportedly produces nothing but counterfeit Marlboro cigarettes. Park explains that the individuals who work in the counterfeit cigarette factories reportedly belong to a special work force team, which entitles them to extra rations — clearly a group that receives much better treatment than the rank-and-file within North Korean society. In an interview conducted recently, Park also explained how several defectors had reported another factory located in the outskirts of Pyongyang that produces counterfeit "Seven" brand cigarettes, one of the most well-known and popular cigarettes consumed legally in South Korea. Of interest, defector reporting indicates the distribution and marketing of counterfeit cigarettes involves networks in other countries, that then enable the cigarettes to be sold throughout Asia. At least some of these networks are reportedly also involved in the distribution of illegal drugs.[46]

According to congressional testimony from State Department official Peter A. Prahar, between 2002 and 2005, counterfeit Marlboro cigarettes were identified in more than 1,300 incidents in the United States. Federal indictments filed in 2006 allege that for several years criminal gangs have arranged for one 40-foot container of North Korea-sourced counterfeit cigarettes per month to enter the United States for illicit sale. Reports from private investigators working abroad on behalf of tobacco corporations state North Korean counterfeit Marlboro cigarettes and other brands are also being sold on a large scale to several countries in the Far East, including Japan and Singapore. As with the sale of illegal drugs, it appears that in the sale of counterfeit cigarettes, the North Koreans are collaborating with Chinese organized crime networks (and likely other networks in the Far East).[47] Japanese and South Korean press reports have cited officials who stated that intelligence data from satellites and Japanese maritime police officials shows North Korea routinely transferred counterfeit cigarettes onto foreign ships registered in Cambodia, Mongolia, and Taiwan. The reports indicated that the cigarettes were counterfeits of American, Japanese, and British tobacco brands. The reports also indicate that due to the size, scope, and relatively low overhead, Pyongyang is possibly drawing in higher profits from counterfeit cigarettes than from other illicit activities.[48]

THE EFFECTS OF 39'S ACTIVITIES

Beyond propping up the North Korean regime and funneling money to its military programs, Office #39's activities create a number of wide-ranging negative effects around the region while undermining international peace and stability. The effects created by these crimes represent another strategic dimension of threats emanating from North Korea. While most of the world is focused on the country's nuclear weapons and related military programs, the criminal acts perpetrated by the regime represent security threats in their own right. Even if the regime were not using these criminal enterprises as a means to contribute to its longevity and to enhance its military capabilities, they would still be viewed as threats that would require a response.

The prolongation of intrastate violence in parts of Asia is an effect of North Korea's drug trafficking. This is most noticeable in the case of Myanmar. North Korea's capacity as a nation-state to facilitate drug running and the acquisition of weapons means that it possesses competitive advantages that the Myanmar guerrillas and Asian organized crime syndicates do not. Insurgent groups in Myanmar produce heroin and methamphetamine for the next node in the trafficking chain, namely the middleman who pays them. As seen with the "guns for drugs" incident, groups in Myanmar do not earn their profits from street sales, but from the middleman that has been, in certain instances, North Korea. Acting as a middleman for Myanmar's guerrillas, North Korea has aided and abetted the ongoing stalemate between certain rebel groups and the government of Myanmar. With arms, and the money to buy arms, these insurgent groups

17

are still able to hold large swathes of territory beyond the central authority of Rangoon. The perpetuation of violence has also led to human rights abuses like the forced recruitment of children soldiers by these guerrilla groups.

North Korea's activities also undermine social stability in a number of other countries through its contacts with violent nonstate actors. For example, Office #39 colluded with Sean Garland, an Official Irish Republican Army head, and leader of the Irish Workers' Party, to run a ring that distributed Supernotes in Belarus, the Czech Republic, Denmark, Great Britain, Ireland, Poland, and Russia.[49] The total proceeds from the ring were estimated to be $28 million. As previously discussed, North Korea also enables organized criminal syndicates like the Japanese Yakuza, Russian Mafiya, and Chinese Triads, to deepen their penetration into illegal markets and erode civil society in their home countries, and in other countries where they operate. It is also believed that North Korea offers safe haven to organized criminal syndicates who provide their expertise to Office #39 and commit crimes in their home countries from the security of a sovereign state.[50]

The growth of poppy crops in North Korea undermines subsistence agriculture in the country and contributes to its recurring famines. These famines have been routinely used by the regime to seek more international humanitarian aid. In some respects, this aid acts as a subsidy for the North Korea opium industry because valuable crop space is not being used to grow food crops. This lack of agricultural development means that the regime cannot rely on the farming sector to generate income for the domestic or export markets, leading to the need to secure hard currency in other more nefarious ways.

North Korea's drug trafficking also contributes to the deterioration of public health in countries where its product is sold. In Japan, it is estimated that somewhere between 40 to 67 percent of methamphetamine comes from North Korea, and has contributed to the rise in the numbers of addicts seeking treatment and rehabilitation.[51] Rising rates of "meth" addiction in Hawaii have also been the result of Korean organized crime groups who have been linked to the North Korean regime.[52]

Money laundering and counterfeiting present another set of problems. Such activities undermine legitimate financial institutions and the legal economies of a number of states. Because the proceeds earned by Office #39 are derived from illicit transactions, they must be concealed in a variety of ways to avoid detection. This involves invoice and licensing fraud, bribery of customs officials, creation of shell companies, and the use of underground or illegal remittance systems. Such wide-ranging involvement means that there are numerous other stakeholders in the activities of Office #39 beyond the regime itself. Citizens and officials from countries like Japan, South Korea, China, Russia, Australia, the United States, Malaysia, Singapore, Taiwan, and Egypt have been swept up in the vortex of North Korea's criminal schemes, contributing to crime rates and, in some cases, the steady erosion of state authority.

Although criminal schemes do represent an additional strategic dimension of threats, of critical concern is the long-standing and ongoing existence of the networks for conducting the illicit activities that Office #39 has put in place. These networks are adaptive, resilient, covert, and widespread; they could be put to use for the transfer of nuclear material from North Korea to other dangerous regimes or to violent nonstate actors. North Korean Vice Minister Kim Kye-gwan warned, "[The United States] should consider the danger that we could transfer nuclear weapons to terrorists, that we have the ability to do so."[53] Even if North Korea does not directly give nuclear weapons or material to a terrorist group, the states that seek nuclear weapons — Iran and Syria — also have money and oil, which the regime needs. In these states, "it would be a short step from the government to some of the sponsored terror groups." [54]

OFFICE #39 AND KIM REGIME SUCCESSION

Criminal sovereignty as conceived and practiced by North Korea is likely to survive the current rule of Kim Jong-il. The "who" that will succeed Kim Jong-il will make a difference to the control of Office #39 and the continuation of criminal sovereignty. That "who" — whether a single individual, a regency that will nurture one of Kim Jong-il's sons, or an oligarchic structure such as the members of the National Defense Commission — will require leadership of those resources that enable control of the military, the KWP, and the internal security apparatus. Keeping these key pieces loyal means control of significant financial assets that Office #39 has been adept at acquiring.

Kim Jong-il's apparent stroke during the summer of 2008[55] demonstrated that Kim's personal rule is nearing its end, and leaves many international leaders and Asian policy analysts wondering who will eventually succeed Kim.[56] Certainly the consequences of that succession process are justification for concern, given North Korea's toxic mixture of economic and social instability and significant military capabilities, including WMD and its ballistic missile arsenal.

Though information about the inner circle leadership is not easy to come by, there are functions within the Kim Regime that one can assess as being consistent with any totalitarian dictatorship[57] — the control of the economy is not the least important for those who rule by force. Central to Kim Jong-il's ability to maintain the financial underpinnings of his totalitarian regime is his creation of a "court economy," akin to that practiced by an absolute monarch.[58] Started in 1972, this court economy predates the emergence of Office #39 but is one of the many drivers of criminal sovereignty. The court economy is responsible for approximately 30 to 40 percent of North Korea's entire economy and is also referred to in a number of other ways, such as the Supreme Leader's economy, the 3rd economy, the elites' economy, the cadre economy, or the party (KWP) economy.[59] The functional heart of this court economy is now, in fact, Office #39.[60]

As discussed earlier, Office #39 has some of its roots in the previous succession process. In preparation for his succession to his father, Kim Il-sung, Kim the younger began a glorification project of his father's rule; this required funding. After being appointed by his father in September 1973 to the two KWP posts of Secretary of the Organization and Guidance Department (OGD), and Secretary of the Propaganda and Agitation Department, Kim Jong-il realized that he needed more effective funding mechanisms to support the regime leadership and his own succession process. Consequently, in 1974 Kim established Office #39 as a separate department within the KWP Secretariat, thus giving Office #39 significant authority. Kim Jong-il has maintained direct supervision over Office #39 since then, while tasking it with the mission of earning foreign currency to fund regime maintenance.[61]

This includes overseeing all of North Korea's foreign transactions;[62] providing funds for Kim Jong-il's personal use;[63] and providing for luxury goods that Kim Jong-il uses to reward the regime's military, government, and party elite;[64] as well as the needs of the regime security agencies.[65] Just as importantly, and more critically for the ongoing Six Party Talks and U.S. policy on North Korea, at least a portion of the foreign currency funds that Office #39 generates for Kim Jong-il go to investing in North Korea's nuclear and missile programs.[66]

The 10 departments in Office #39 specialize in all types of material goods, giving the next North Korean leader(s) access to specialized transactions in support of his/their activities, especially important during the power consolidation phase after Kim Jong-il's death. In support of these activities, and organizationally subordinate to the Daesung General Bureau, are the Daesung Bank, the Kyunghung Guidance Bureau, the Nakwon Guidance Bureau, the Kumgang Guidance Bureau, and the Daehung Guidance Bureau.[67] Interestingly, the profits from all of these Office #39 elements, as well as those subordinate to other party and military functions, are only presented (under the pretext of "revolutionary funds") in large aggregate sums to Kim Jong-il on special occasions such as his birthday on February 12, Kim Il-sung's birthday on April 15, New Year's Day, and other important dates of the North Korean calendar. Under what pretext and under what name will these same funds be presented to the next North Korean leader(s)? Changing this presentation formula by Office #39 could lead to complications in the trust factor among the regime elite, and could seriously jeopardize the financial underpinnings of the regime.

One of the natural questions for all regional leaders and political analysts is: Who will control Office #39 and the foreign currency that makes the Kim Regime run once Kim Jong-il is dead or no longer capable of controlling the regime or governing the country? Considering Office #39's role in providing financial support to regime functions, control of it gives Kim Jong-il's successor(s) the ability to fund rewards for the regime elite, significant control over North Korea's illicit activities, and at least financial influence over North Korea's WMD programs. Such influence is considerable, considering Office #39's operating principles.

There are a number of individuals who are in positions to control Office #39 after Kim Jong-il is no longer able to govern or has died. The military maintains a monopoly on the guns, and the National Defense Commission is the governing apparatus of the state. Furthermore, the military elite have their own trading companies and banks to conduct foreign currency earnings. But the military elite ultimately come under the control of the party through the General Political Bureau, which reports directly to Kim Jong-il through the very powerful Organization and Guidance Department. Though Kim Jong-il has apparently appointed his third son, Kim Jong-un, as his heir apparent,[68] one individual stands out distinctly from all others in terms of his widespread influence within the OGD — Kim Jong-il's brother-in-law, Chang Sung-taek.[69] Chang is one of four First Vice-Directors of the OGD, one of four seconds to Kim Jong-il's position as OGD Secretary (arguably the most powerful office Kim uses to control the regime's elite). Chang is personally responsible for oversight of the internal security agencies[70] that maintain vigilance over the political reliability of every single North Korean citizen. In addition to his First Vice-Director position, Chang also supervises the OGD's Party Headquarters Department, a position from which he maintains significant influence over Office #39 personnel. Also, in addition to being a Kim Regime family member by virtue of his marriage to Kim Jong-il's only full-blooded relative, his sister Kim Kyung-hui, Chang was recently appointed to the National Defense Commission (NDC).[71] Though not a military man, from this position Chang will be able to review military policy and national-level decisionmaking within the NDC. From these positions of influence, Chang should be able to use the significant financial resources of Office #39 to influence other members of the NDC (most importantly), and other regime elite, to ensure either the succession of Kim Jong-il's third son by acting as regent, or even move to make himself leader of North Korea (though the sum efforts of the other NDC members would likely prevent this). The resources that Office #39 provides not only gives the next leader domestic influence, but financially supports at least a portion of North Korea's WMD programs—with corresponding influence over foreign policy.

Whoever leads North Korea next will control the operations of Office #39 and thus influence the other regime elite, while maintaining Office #39's 17 overseas offices, including Moscow, Beijing, Hong Kong, and Singapore. The next leader will also control Office #39's representative offices at every major sea port and rail junction in North Korea.[72] Office #39 also maintains liaison offices in every province, city, and county in North Korea.[73] The next North Korean leader will also control Office #39's largest operating agency, the Daesung General Bureau, under which are numerous subordinate trade companies and foreign exchange banks, all independent of the North Korean state and ultimately following only the guidance of Kim Jong-il through the KWP's Organization and Guidance Department.[74] Whoever succeeds Kim Jong-il as the OGD Party Secretary will have control over all aspects of Office #39, particularly the careers of every single employee of the bureau.[75] Founded on May 6, 1974, the Daesung General Bureau has grown so large that Office #39 and all of its subordinate organizations have become known within North Korea as the Daesung Conglomerate.[76] This conglomerate, which in many ways is far more influential than, for example, South Korea's major conglomerates of Samsung, Hyundai, and Daewoo, and which is tasked by Kim Jong-il with providing every kind of goods — industrial, agricultural, marine, and technical, both domestic and foreign, and both through legitimate and illicit venues — has numerous trading companies and exchange banks that the next North Korean leader(s) can use to conduct its foreign currency earnings overseas and domestically.

RECOMMENDATIONS

How can criminal sovereignty as practiced by North Korea be confronted? It is important to underscore that North Korea is not an ordinary nation-state that uses sovereignty to protect its citizens, conducts benign relations with other nation-states, or sees criminal activities as corrosive to the international order. For North Korea, sovereignty is used to shield the regime from intrusive acts that may compromise its externally directed criminal activities and which are perpetrated by the organs, institutions, and personnel of the government itself. Coming to grips with such a complex state requires multifaceted approaches.

- Do not view illegal activities as contingent upon North Korea's military ambitions. North Korea would likely continue its criminal enterprises even in the event of successful nuclear disarmament. The North Korean elite, including senior members of the military, need hard currency to continue to maintain their power. Because this organization was not only established by the current leader of North Korea, but also proven to be extremely profitable for its duration, it is likely that Kim Jong-il will be extremely hesitant to dismantle the programs that come under its umbrella.

- Sanctions on North Korea can create pain for the regime, but they will not force an end to the country's criminal schemes. Sanctions were aimed at gaining North Korean concessions at the nuclear negotiating table. They were not aimed at stopping the regime's criminal conduct. In fact, the United States unfroze North Korean assets gained from criminal acts as a way to make progress on the prospects for nuclear disarmament and after North Korea promised to use the money for humanitarian purposes.

- Crackdowns during 2005-07 by the U.S. Treasury Department on front companies and banks either owned by the North Koreans or used by them (that were conducting illegal activities) apparently caused significant damage to Pyongyang's illicit economic networks. Recent resumption of these crackdowns may again threaten the viability of these networks — and can be enhanced by cooperation from allies.

- North Korea should not be described as a nation-state that is simply misbehaving. North Korea engages in criminality not as a matter of choice, but of necessity. Its reliance on illicit activities is not likely to be eased by offering inducements or increasing sanctions. Real change in behavior can only happen from the top, and an analysis of the succession process indicates that those who succeed Kim Jong-il are unlikely to cease Pyongyang's illicit activities.
- States in the region should work to strengthen law enforcement cooperation. The Proliferation Security Initiative has made important strides in this direction, but it is mainly directed towards North Korea's arms trade. Because of the wide ranging nature of Office #39's crimes and their effects, law enforcement from a number of countries should establish "fusion centers" dedicated specifically to tracking North Korean illicit activities.
- Expand United Nations (UN) Security Council Resolution 1874. Following North Korea's long-range ballistic missile test and underground nuclear test in 2009, the UN Security Council issued sanctions that targeted not only North Korean financial institutions, but key individuals associated with nuclear, ballistic missile, and other WMD-related programs or activities. This can and should be expanded to include front companies and individuals engaged in counterfeiting, drug trafficking, money laundering, and other illicit activities that support the Democratic People's Republic of Korea (DPRK) regime and pose a threat to the national security of nations in the region and elsewhere.

CONCLUSION

Criminal sovereignty is an unusual practice in international relations. North Korea has been practicing it for decades; it is unlikely that it can be successfully ended in the short term. North Korea has proven to be creative at adapting state power for criminal purposes that are directed externally for the purposes of regime survival and military progress. Criminal sovereignty may still take a number of new forms in the future. Office #39's activities have evolved and continue to do so, meaning that policymakers should exercise ever more vigilance in analyzing, assessing, and challenging North Korea's behavior.

ENDNOTES

1. See Selig Harrison, *Korean Endgame: A Strategy for Reunification and U.S. Disengagement*, Princeton, NJ: Princeton University Press, 2002, p. 311.

2. Phar Kim Beng, "Shady Business: North Korea and Crime," *Asia Times*, November 30, 2004, available from *www.atimes.com/atimes/printN.html*.

3. For more on how this culture of "fear of attack" exists in North Korea, see Jill Dougherty, "North Korea: A prism to Soviet era," *CNN.Com*, June 19, 2008, available from *edition.cnn.com/2008/WORLD/asiapcf/06/19/nkorea.dougherty.notebook/index.html*.

4. Todd Crowell, "North Korea: The 'Sopranos' State," *Asia Times Online*, January 18, 2006, available from *www.atimes.com/atimes/Korea/HA18Dg01.html*; and Bill Powell and Adam Zagorin, "The Tony Soprano of North Korea," *time.com*, July 12, 2007, available from *www.time.com/time/magazine/article/0,9171,1642898,00.html*.

5. For more detailed analysis on the large-scale subsidies that the Soviet Union provided North Korea during the 1970s, see Nicholas Eberstadt, "The Persistence of North Korea," *Policy Review*, No. 127, October and November 2004, available from *www.policyreview.org/oct04/eberstadt.html*.

6. Anthony LoBaido, "N. Korea's Slush Fund: Dictator Reportedly Stashed $2 billion in Austrian Bank," *World Net Daily*, March 19, 2000, available from *www.worldnetdaily.com/news/article.asp?ARTICLE_ID=19068*.

7. For detailed analysis of Kim Jong-il's gradual rise to power under his father's guidance, see Alexandre Y. Mansourov, "Inside North Korea's Black Box: Reversing the Optics," *Brookings Institution Paper*, June 2004, available from *www.brookings.edu/views/papers/fellows/oh20040601ch4.pdf*.

8. See Kim Kwang-jin, "The Dollarization of the North Korean Economy and Kim Chong-il's Court Economy," *Tongil Yongu* (Unification Research), Vol. 11, No. 2, 2007 (in Korean).

9. Anthony Spaeth, "Kim's Rackets: To Fund His Lifestyle — and His Nukes — Kim Jong Il Helms a Vast Criminal Network," June 2, 2003, available from *www.time.com/time/asia/covers/501030609/story.html*.

10. Mike Chinoy, "Will China End North Korea's Illegal Activities in Macao?" *CNN.Com*, December 18, 1999, available from *archives.cnn.com/1999/ASIANOW/east/macau/stories/macau.north.korea/index.html*.

11. Jay Solomon and Hae Won Choi, "Money Trail: In North Korea, Secret Cash Hoard Props Up Regime," *Wall Street Journal*, July 14, 2003, p. A01.

12. "N. Korean Leader Moved Secret Bank Accounts to Luxembourg: Report," *Yonhap*, December 27, 2005, available from *english.yna.co.kr/Engnews/20051227/430100000020051227194320E2.html*.

13. "Singapore: N. Korea's New Money Haven," *Donga Ilbo*, August 5, 2006, available from *english.donga.com/srv/service.php3?bicode=060000&biid=2006080539518*.

14. Barbara Demick, "No More Gambling on N. Korea," *Los Angeles Times*, April 6, 2006, available from *www.latimes.com/news/printedition/la-fg-macao6apr06,1,7483991.story*.

15. Spaeth.

16. Jay Solomon and Jason Dean, "Heroin Busts Point to Source of Funds for North Koreans," *Wall Street Journal*, April 23, 2003.

17. Kim Young-il, "North Korea and Narcotics Trafficking: A View from the Inside," *North Korean Review*, Vol. 1, Issue 1, February 2009, available from *www.jamestown.org/single/?no_cache=1&tx_ttnews%5Btt_news%5D=26320*.

18. Life Inside North Korea: Hearings before the Senate Subcommittee on East Asian and Pacific Affairs of the Committee of Foreign Relations, 108th Cong., 1st Sess., June 5, 2003, p. 12.

19. Solomon and Dean.

20. *Ibid.*

21. Bertil Lintner and Shawn Crispin, "For US, New North Korea Problem," *Wall Street Journal*, November 18, 2003.

22. "Drugs, Counterfeiting, and Weapons Proliferation: The North Korean Connection," Hearings before the Senate Financial Management, Budget, and International Subcommittee of the Committee on Governmental Affairs, 108th Cong., 1st Sess., May 20, 2003, p. 16.

23. Solomon and Dean.

24. Balbina Hwang, "Curtailing North Korea's Illicit Activities," *Backgrounder*, No. 1679, Washington, DC: Heritage Foundation, August 25, 2003, p. 8.

25. *Ibid.*

26. Bertil Litner, *Blood Brothers: The Criminal Underworld of Asia,* New York: Palgrave MacMillan, 2003.

27. Sheena E. Chestnut, "Sopranos State? North Korean Involvement in Criminal Activity and Implications for International Security," *Nautilus Institute Special Report,* San Francisco, CA: The Nautilus Institute, January 19, 2006 p. 109., available from *www.nautilus.org/napsnet/sr/2006/0605Chestnut.pdf.*

28. Cindy A. Hurst, "North Korea: Government Sponsored Drug Trafficking," *Military Review,* September-October, 2005, available from *libweb.uoregon.edu/ec/e-asia/read/NK-drugs.pdf.*

29. Ah-Young Kim, "End North Korea's Drug Trade," *Pacific Forum CSIS,* No. 26, June 13, 2003, available from *csis.org/files/media/csis/pubs/pac0326.pdf.*

30. Hurst.

31. "North Koreans Relocate out of Macau," *JoongAng Ilbo,* July 7, 2009, available from *www.cacda.org.cn/english/news/Read.asp?ID=1180.*

32. Miwa Murphy, "Knowledge, Not Speculation, Key to North Korea, Experts Says," *Japan Times,* February 23, 2006.

33. "Treasury Designates Banco Delta Asia as Primary Money Laundering Concern under USA PATRIOT Act," United *States Department of Treasury Press Release,* September 15, 2005, available from *www.treas.gov/press/releases/js2720.htm.*

34. Chestnut, p. 82.

35. Congressman Ed Royce, "Gangster Regime: How North Korea Counterfeits United States Currency," *Staff Report,* Washington, DC: U.S. House of Representative, March 12, 2007, available from *www.royce.house.gov/uploadedfiles/report.3.12.07.FINAL.GansterRegime.pdf.*

36. Josh Meyer and Barbara Demick, "Counterfeiting Cases Point to North Korea," *Los Angeles Times,* December 12, 2005, available from *www.tobacco.org/scripts/jump.php?article_*

id=212369&url=www.latimes.com/news/printedition/la-fg-counterfeit 12dec12,1,1659491,full.story.

37. "Defectors: Counterfeit Bills Printed at Press in Pyeongseong, North Korea," *East Asia Intel*, December 7, 2005, available from *www.east-asia-intel.com/eai/2005/12_07/4.asp.*

38. Bill Gertz, "N. Korea Charged in Counterfeiting of U.S. Currency," *Washington Times*, December 2, 2005, available from *www.washingtontimes.com/world/20051201-103509-5867r.htm.*

39. David Samuels, "Counterfeiting: Notes on a Scandal," *The Independent*, August 24, 2009, available from *www.independent. co.uk/news/world/asia/counterfeiting-notes-on-a-scandal-1776329. html.*

40. "N. Korean Supernotes Surfaced In Las Vegas Casinos," *East-Asia-Intel.Com*, January 11, 2006, available from *www.east-asia-intel.com/eai/2006/01_11/3.asp.*

41. David Rose, "North Korea's Dollar Store," *Vanity Fair*, August 5, 2009, available from *www.vanityfair.com/politics/ features/2009/09/office-39-200909.*

42. "China Finds N. Korea Guilty of Money Laundering," *Chosun Ilbo*, January 11, 2006, available from *english.chosun.com/ w21data/html/news/200601/200601110019.html.*

43. "N.K. Counterfeit Bill Accounts Surface in Hong Kong," *Chosun Ilbo*, February 27, 2006, *english.chosun.com/w21data/html/ news/200602/200602270018.html.*

44. See "China Cracks Down on Counterfeit Dollars," *Chosun Ilbo*, March 19, 2006, *english.chosun.com/w21data/html/ news/200603/200603190006.html*; Gordon Fairclough, "North Korea Might Be Exporting Fake $100 Bills," *Wall Street Journal*, March 24, 2006, available from *www.washingtonpost.com/wp-dyn/ content/article/2006/03/23/AR2006032301534.html.*

45. David Asher, "The North Korean Criminal State, Its Ties to Organized Crime, and the Possibility of WMD Proliferation," San Francisco, CA: Nautilus Institute, Policy Forum Online 05-

92A, November 15, 2005, available from *www.nautilus.org/fora/ security/0502Asher.html.*

46. Park Syung-je, Board Member, Military Analyst Association of the Republic of Korea, Seoul, Republic of Korea, email interviews by Bruce E. Bechtol, Jr., on January 22, 2006, and September 10, 2009.

47. Peter A. Prahar, Director, Office of African, Asia and Europe/NIS Programs, Bureau for International Narcotics and Law Enforcement Affairs, Department of State, "Prepared Statement: North Korea: Illicit Activity Funding the Regime," Senate Sub-Committee on Financial Management, Government Information, and International Security, Senate Homeland Security and Government Affairs Committee, April 25, 2006, available from *hsgac.senate.gov/_files/042506Prahar.pdf.*

48. See Yeh Young-june, "Report: North Ships Caught with Fake Cigarettes," *Joongang Ilbo,* May 16, 2006, available from *joongangdaily.joins.com/200605/15/200605152229094209900090309 031.html;* "Vessels from NK Carry Fake Cigarettes," *KBS World Radio,* May 15, 2006, available from *world.kbs.co.kr/english/news/ news_detail.htm?No=36221.*

49. Sheena Chestnut, "Illicit Activity and Proliferation," *International Security,* Summer 2007, p. 91.

50. David Asher, "North Korea—Illicit Activity Funding the Regime," Hearing before the Senate Homeland Security and Governmental Affairs Subcommittee on Federal Financial Management, 109th Cong., 2d Sess., April 25, 2006.

51. Spaeth.

52. Information Bulletin: Crystal Methamphetamine, National Drug Intelligence Center, August 12, 2002, available from *www. usdoj.gov/ndic/pubs1/1837/index.htm.*

53. Selig Harrison, "North Korea Warns of Nuke Proliferations Possibility: US Scholar," Kyodo News Service, April 9, 2005.

54. Chestnut, "Illicit Activity and Proliteration." p. 103.

55. See "Kim Jong-il Possibly Suffered a Stroke: US Intelligence," *AFP*, September 9, 2008, available from *afp.google. com/article/ALeqM5hI60aOG6LVdVj_ZBf9hguvfoQRWA*; Steven Erlanger, "Doctor Confirms Kim Jong-il Stroke," *The New York Times*, December 11, 2008, available from *www.nytimes. com/2008/12/12/world/asia/12kim.html*; "Western Officials Say North Korean Leader Kim Jong Il May Have Suffered Stroke," *FOXNEWS*, September 09, 2008, available from *www.foxnews.com/ story/0,2933,419263,00.html*..

56. See North Korea Confirms It Has Nuclear Weapons, *FOXNEWS*, February 11, 2005, available from *www.foxnews.com/ story/0,2933,146950,00.html*; Justin McCurry and Tania Branigan, "North Korea Tests Nuclear Weapon 'As Powerful As Hiroshima Bomb" *The Guardian*, May 25, 2009, available from *www.guardian. co.uk/world/2009/may/25/north-korea-hiroshima-nuclear-test*.

57. For a detailed analysis of Kim Jong-il's totalitarian approach to ruling North Korea, see Park Hyung-jung *et al.*, "The North Korean Political System Under Kim Jong-il: Continuity and Change in Ruling Ideology, Authority Elites, and Authority Structure," Seoul, Korea: Korean Institute for National Unification, 2004 (in Korean).

58. See Vasily Mikheev, "Reforms of the North Korean Economy: Requirements, Plans and Hopes," *The Korean Journal of Defense Analysis*, Vol. V, No. 1, Summer 1993, pp. 81-95.

59. See Kim Kwang-jin, "Study on Changes to the North Korea's Foreign Exchange System," Seoul, Korea: Graduate School of North Korean Studies, Master's Thesis, December 2007, p. 23 (in Korean).

60. *Ibid*. Also see *Encyclopedia of North Korea* (1993-2002), Detroit, MI: University of Detroit Mercy, Institute for North Korean Studies, June 2003, p. 218 (in Korean); Jung Kwang-min, "The Political Economy of the North Korean Famine," Seoul, Korea: Sidae Jungsin Publishers, 2005 (in Korean).

61. Kim Kwang-jin, "The Dollarization of the North Korean Economy and Kim Chong-il's Court Economy."

62. See Kang Myung-Do, "Dreams of Exile From Pyongyang," Seoul, Korea: Choson Ilbo Publishers, 1995, p.160 (in Korean); Kim Kwang-jin, "Study on Changes to the North Korea's Foreign Exchange System," p.75.

63. See Kim Kwang-jin, "Study on Changes to the North Korea's Foreign Exchange System," p. 65.

64. See Hyun Seong-il, "North Korea's National Strategy and Power Elites: Focus on Cadre Policy," Seoul, Korea: Sonin Publishers, 2007, pp. 361-396 (in Korean).

65. See Hwang Jang-yop, "I Have Seen the Truth of History," Seoul, Korea: Hanjul Publishing, 1999, pp. 184-185 (in Korean).

66. See Kim Kwang-jin, "Kim Chong-il's Court Economy is Destroying the National Economy," *Sidae Jungsin Journal,* Summer 2008 (in Korean), available from *www.sdjs.co.kr.*

67. *Ibid.*

68. See Jack Kim, "North Korea leader picks 3rd son as heir: media," *Reuters,* January 15, 2009, available from *www.reuters. com/article/topnews/idustre50e2hf20090115?feedtype=rrs&feedname= topnews*; Kim Sue-young and Michael Ha, "Kim Jong-il's 3rd Son Emerges as Successor," *Korea Times,* January 15, 2009, available from *www.koreatimes.co.kr/www/news/nation/2009/01/117_37961. html.*

69. See "Kim's Brother-in-Law Said to Mastermind N.Korea's Leadership Succession," *Yonhap,* February 15, 2009, available from *english.yonhapnews.co.kr/northkorea/2009/02/15/0401000000a en20090215001900315.html.*

70. The most powerful of these agencies are the State Security Department and the Ministry of People's Security.

71. See Philippa Fogarty, "Profile: Chang Song-taek," *BBC News,* April 21, 2009, available from *news.bbc.co.uk/2/hi/ americas/8002562.stm.*

72. *Ibid.*

73. *Ibid.*

74. The OGD is arguably the most powerful organization within North Korea. Kim Jong-il has served as its Party Secretary since 1973.

75. See Hyun Seong-il, pp. 105-130.

76. See Kim Kwang-jin, "Study on Changes to the North Korea's Foreign Exchange System," p. 75.

U.S. ARMY WAR COLLEGE

Major General Robert M. Williams
Commandant

*****

STRATEGIC STUDIES INSTITUTE

Director
Professor Douglas C. Lovelace, Jr.

Director of Research
Dr. Antulio J. Echevarria II

Authors
Dr. Paul Rexton Kan
Dr. Bruce E. Bechtol, Jr.
Mr. Robert M. Collins

Director of Publications
Dr. James G. Pierce

Publications Assistant
Ms. Rita A. Rummel

*****

Composition
Mrs. Jennifer E. Nevil